Prolance

www.prolancewriting.com
California, USA
©2017 Hirrah Khan
Illustrations ©2017 Marina Adam

ISBN: 978-0-9987527-0-9

Love at First Sight

A father's tale of loss and love

Written by Hirrah Khan
Illustrated by Marina Adam

PROLANCE

Dedication

I would like to dedicate this book
to my dear husband, Qasim Aazar
and to all the fathers who have
been on a journey of loss and love.

Tiny little hands and tiny little toes.
They peeked into this world with a beautiful glow.

Azmaira came first.
Then Zainab followed with a burst.

Baba was so glad to greet them.
He couldn't take his eyes off his two gems.

He held them both very close to his heart.
And looked into their eyes to see if he could tell them apart.

Azmaira resembled Mama.
Zainab mirrored Baba.

The four of them together created the perfect family photo.

Little round faces.
Pointy little noses.
Oh so soft skin.
And perfect tiny poses.

Baba tried to take his eyes off of them with all his might.
After all, it was love at first sight.

Baba did not know he could love his daughters so much.
It felt like his heart grew because of their touch.

In moments, it all froze.
The clock stopped ticking and everyone paused.

Then time resumed.
The sun continued to set and the clock started ticking again.

Azmaira and Zainab said to Mama and Baba, "It's time for us to go."
Baba and Mama got worried.
They didn't want their precious babies to go.

But Azmaira and Zainab explained,
"Don't worry! We will meet again very soon.
In a place where everything will be as bright as
the moon."

Before Azmaira and Zainab said good-bye, they whispered,
"Please don't cry."
"Even though we cannot stay, we will still be with you everyday."
Baba and Mama kissed them good-bye.
With salty tears in their eyes.

Although Azmaira and Zainab were now gone.
Mama and Baba were left with a piece of their heart to carry on.

Azmaira and Zainab will always be a part of them.
Forever, their two little gems.

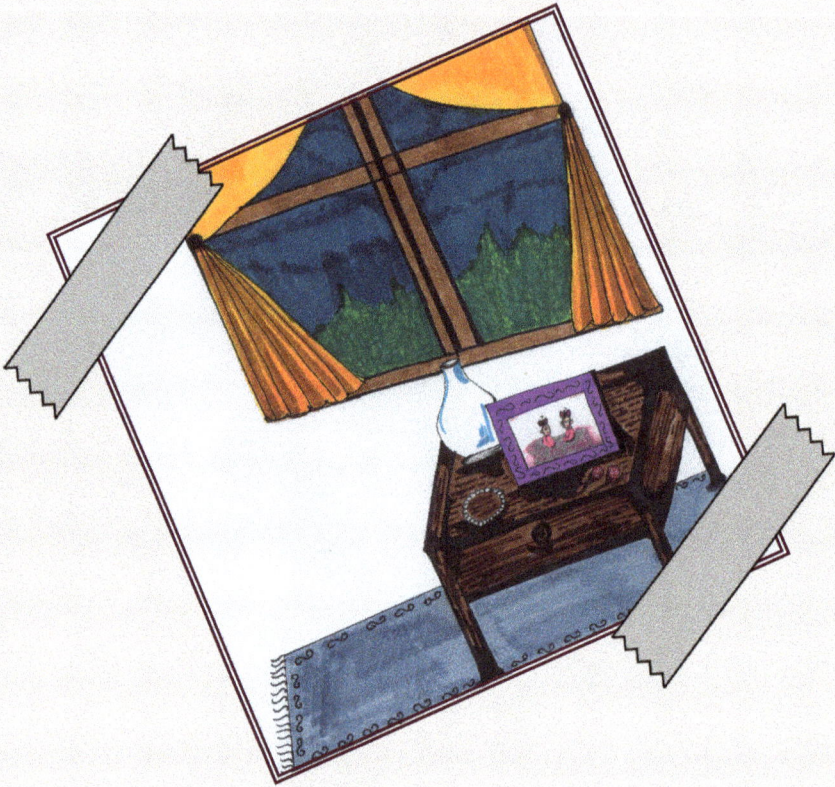

They taught them patience.
They taught them strength.
They taught them love is greater than sorrow's length.

Time has passed, and the sun shines bright.
But even today, Baba stands still at night thinking of his girls
...his love at first sight!

Hirrah Khan's new-found passion for writing encouraged her to write about her family's journey of loss and love. She lives in Mississauga, Ontario. Hirrah is a teacher by profession and also enjoys to blog about motherhood every once in a while. She feels that through writing she can keep the short-lived memories of her twin daughters alive.

www.ingramcontent.com/pod-product-compliance
Lightning Source LLC
Chambersburg PA
CBHW041634040426
42447CB00020B/3493